THE
STUDENT
COOKBOOK

COOKING FOR THE STUDENT LIFE!

First published in 2013
LOVE FOOD is an imprint of Parragon Books Ltd

Parragon
Chartist House
15–17 Trim Street
Bath, BA1 1HA, UK

www.parragon.com/lovefood

ISBN: 978-1-4723-0288-5

Printed in China

Notes for the Reader
This book uses standard kitchen measuring spoons and cups. All spoon and cup measurements are
level unless otherwise indicated. Unless otherwise stated, milk is assumed to be whole, eggs are large,
individual vegetables are medium, and pepper is freshly ground black pepper. Unless otherwise stated,
all root vegetables should be washed in plain water and peeled prior to using.

For the best results, use a meat thermometer when cooking meat and poultry—check the latest
USDA government guidelines for current advice.

Garnishes and serving suggestions are all optional and not necessarily included in the recipe ingredients
or method. The times given are only an approximate guide. Preparation times differ according to the
techniques used by different people and the cooking times may also vary from those given. Optional
ingredients, variations, or serving suggestions have not been included in the calculations.

Recipes using raw or very lightly cooked eggs should be avoided by infants, the elderly, pregnant
women, and people with weakened immune systems. Pregnant and breast-feeding women are advised
to avoid eating peanuts and peanut products. People with nut allergies should be aware that some of
the prepared ingredients used in the recipes in this book may contain nuts. Always check the packaging
before use.

Vegetarians should be aware that some of the prepared ingredients used in the recipes in this book may
contain animal products. Always check the package before use.

CONTENTS

SUNSHINE TOAST 6

CHIVE SCRAMBLED EGGS 8

APPLE PANCAKES (WITH MAPLE SYRUP BUTTER) 10

DELI-STYLE SANDWICHES 12

TURKEY SALAD PITA POCKETS 14

NACHOS 16

PASTA SALAD 18

VEGETABLE FAJITAS 20

CHICKEN SKEWERS (WITH SATAY SAUCE) 22

YAKISOBA 24

CHICKEN NUGGETS 28

CLASSIC CHEESEBURGERS 30

THIN CRUST PIZZA (WITH VEG AND MOZZARELLA) 32

MACARONI & CHEESE 34

TUNA-NOODLE CASSEROLE 36

CHILI CON CARNE 38

SPAGHETTI WITH MEATBALLS 40

NO-BAKE CHOCOLATE CAKE 42

PEANUT BUTTER COOKIES 44

BAKED BANANAS (WITH CHOCOLATE SAUCE) 46

INDEX 48

PLUS!
TIPS FOR SHOPPING
ON A BUDGET
PAGE 26

INTRODUCTION

So, you've finally done it. You've left home and are standing on your own two feet. Congratulations—you've become a student. The hallowed halls and classrooms of academia are calling, a wide world of learning beckons. Well, something like that anyway.

Going to college is not just about libraries, labs, and lectures. Let's be honest—if it was, the whole thing wouldn't be half as much fun. The real highlight of student life is what happens when you're away from your books. These years are about leaving the comforts (and restrictions) of home and experiencing stuff for yourself. There will be clubs to join, teams to get involved with. There's a (very) good chance the Union cafeteria will become a place you're intimately familiar with. There will be an indecent number of parties and an embarrassing number of nights out. Over the next four years, you're going to have a better, more active, more exciting social diary than you will ever experience again. In other words, you're going to have the time of your life.

Once you reach college, Mom's three square meals a day will become a distant memory, and unless you learn your way around a kitchen, you're going to be pretty hungry. However, don't be intimidated. It's easier than you think. As the recipes that follow show, a repertoire of simple, wholesome, well-prepared meals will be just as impressive as a wonderfully complicated, solitary cordon bleu creation. With a little practice, you'll soon be making food that looks and smells so good, you won't know whether to eat it or kiss it!

The student kitchen can be a lot more than a place to make some coffee or scrounge some toast; it can be the center of your away-from-home life. Cooking for your roommates will forge strong bonds—but you should make sure you get a few free meals back, too. Most of all, it's fun! So grab an apron, get cooking, and dig in. Trust us: There's really nothing like some home cooking for finally shaking off the effects of being up too late the night before.

SUNSHINE TOAST

Serves: 1

Prep: 5 mins

Cook: 10–12 mins

1 slice whole-grain or
   whole-wheat bread
1 tablespoon olive oil
2–3 mushrooms,
   sliced
1 tomato, halved
1 medium egg
pepper, to taste

1 Very lightly toast the bread in a toaster or under a broiler. Using a cookie cutter, cut a hole in the center of the slice of toast, large enough to hold the egg.

2 Heat the oil in a nonstick skillet and cook the mushrooms and tomato, cut sides down, for 3–4 minutes, until the mushrooms are beginning to brown. Turn the tomato over.

3 Make a space in the middle of the skillet and add the toast. Crack the egg into a small bowl and carefully pour it into the hole in the toast. Reduce the heat and cook slowly until cooked through.

4 Season with pepper, then transfer the toast, mushrooms, and tomato to a plate and serve immediately.

This hearty breakfast dish is quick, tasty, and ideal for those who hate cleaning up—it uses only one pan.

CHIVE SCRAMBLED EGGS

Serves: 2

Prep: 5 mins

Cook: 8–10 mins

4 eggs
½ cup light cream
2 tablespoons
  snipped fresh
  chives, plus extra
  to garnish
2 tablespoons butter
4 slices bread
salt and pepper,
  to taste

1 Break the eggs into a medium bowl and whisk gently with the cream. Season with salt and pepper and add the snipped chives.

2 Melt the butter in a skillet and pour in the egg mixture. Let set slightly, then move the mixture toward the center of the skillet, using a wooden spoon, as the eggs begin to cook. Continue in this way until the eggs are cooked but still creamy.

3 Lightly toast the bread in a toaster or under a broiler and place on plates. Spoon the scrambled eggs on top of the toast, garnish with chives, and serve immediately.

Try adding some smoked salmon to this dish for a special take on scrambled eggs.

APPLE PANCAKES
(with maple syrup butter)

Serves: 4–6

Prep: 5 mins

Cook: 10–12 mins

1½ cups all-purpose
  flour
½ cup granulated
  sugar
2 teaspoons baking
  powder
1 teaspoon ground
  cinnamon
1 egg
1 cup milk
2 apples, peeled
  and grated
1 teaspoon butter

Maple syrup butter
6 tablespoons butter,
  softened
3 tablespoons
  maple syrup

1. To make the pancakes, mix together the flour, sugar, baking powder, and cinnamon in a bowl and make a well in the center. Beat together the egg and milk and pour into the well. Using a wooden spoon, gently incorporate the dry ingredients into the liquid, then stir in the grated apple.

2. Heat the butter in a large nonstick skillet over low heat until bubbling. Add tablespoons of the pancake batter to form 3½-inch circles. Cook each pancake for about 1 minute, until it starts to bubble lightly on the top and looks set, then flip it over and cook the other side for 30 seconds, or until cooked through. The pancakes should be golden brown; if not, increase the heat a little. Remove from the skillet and keep warm. Repeat until all the pancake batter has been used.

3. To make the maple syrup butter, melt the butter with the maple syrup in a saucepan over low heat and stir until combined. To serve, place the pancakes on serving dishes and spoon the flavored butter over the top. Serve warm.

DELI-STYLE SANDWICHES

Serves: 2

Prep: 5 mins

Cook: No cooking

4 slices rye,
   pumpernickel, or
   whole-grain bread
mayonnaise,
   margarine, or
   butter, softened,
   for spreading
2 teaspoons yellow
   mustard
2–4 slices Swiss
   cheese
8–10 slices pastrami
2–4 pickles, sliced
¼ cup coleslaw
potato chips, to serve

1 Lightly spread the slices of bread with mayonnaise, margarine, or butter, then spread with the mustard.

2 Divide the cheese slices equally between the top of two of the bread slices, then place the pastrami slices loosely on top. Add the sliced pickles and coleslaw to each sandwich and top with the remaining bread slices.

3 Place each sandwich on a serving plate and cut in half with a sharp knife. Serve with potato chips on the side.

Try these Rueben-style sandwiches for a less-expensive—and healthier—alternative to sandwiches from a delicatessen.

TURKEY SALAD PITA POCKETS

 Serves: 1

Prep: 5 mins

Cook: 2 mins

small handful baby
 leaf spinach, rinsed,
 patted dry, and
 shredded
½ red bell pepper,
 seeded and thinly
 sliced
½ carrot, peeled and
 coarsely shredded
¼ cup hummus
a few slices deli
 turkey, cut into
 strips
½ tablespoon
 sunflower seeds
1 whole-wheat pita
 bread
salt and pepper,
 to taste

1 Put the spinach leaves, red bell pepper, carrot, and hummus into a large bowl and stir together until all the salad ingredients are coated with the hummus. Stir in the turkey and sunflower seeds and season with salt and pepper.

2 Preheat the broiler to high. Broil the pita bread for about 1 minute on each side to warm through, but do not brown. Cut it in half to make two "pockets" of bread.

3 Divide the filling between the pita bread pockets and serve immediately.

Mix and match your fillings for these delicious pita pockets with sliced chicken or ham and some shredded cheese.

NACHOS

Serves: 6

Prep: 10 mins

Cook: 5–8 mins

---

6 ounces tortilla chips
1 (16-ounce) can
  refried beans,
  warmed
2 tablespoons finely
  chopped jalapeño
  chilies from a jar
1 cup canned
  pimentos or roasted
  peppers, drained
  and finely sliced
1 cup shredded
  Monterey Jack
  cheese
1 cup shredded
  cheddar cheese
salt and pepper,
  to taste

1 Preheat the oven to 400°F.

2 Spread the tortilla chips out over the
bottom of a large, shallow, ovenproof dish
or roasting pan. Cover with the warmed
refried beans. Scatter with the chilies and
pimentos and season with salt and pepper.
Mix the cheeses together in a bowl
and sprinkle on top.

3 Bake in the preheated oven for 5–8 minutes,
or until the cheese is bubbling and melted.
Serve immediately.

Perfect for parties or gatherings
with friends, these irresistible
nachos feed a lot of people for
very little money.

PASTA SALAD

Serves: 2

Prep: 10 mins

Cook: 10–15 mins

4 ounces dried pasta shapes
1 tablespoon olive oil, plus extra if needed
1 (5-ounce) can chunk light tuna in oil, drained and flaked
1 cup drained corn kernels
2 tomatoes, peeled, seeded, and diced
½ green bell pepper, seeded and chopped
½ avocado, pitted, peeled, and chopped

Dressing
1 tablespoon mayonnaise
1 tablespoon plain yogurt
2 tablespoons pesto
pinch of salt
pepper

1. Bring a large saucepan of lightly salted water to a boil. Add the pasta, bring back to a boil, and cook according to the package directions. Drain, return the pasta to the pan, and add the oil. Toss well to coat, then cover and let cool.

2. To make the dressing, whisk together the mayonnaise, yogurt, and pesto in a small bowl, adding a little oil, if needed, to achieve the desired consistency. Add a pinch of salt and season with pepper.

3. Mix the cooled pasta with the tuna, corn, tomatoes, green bell pepper, and avocado, add the dressing, and toss well to coat. Serve immediately.

This delicious pasta salad is light, healthy and easily packed in a plastic box container for an appetizing lunch on the run.

VEGETABLE FAJITAS

Serves: 4–8

Prep: 10 mins

Cook: 12–15 mins

1 pound large, flat
  mushrooms
2 tablespoons oil
1 onion, sliced
1 red bell pepper,
  seeded and sliced
1 green bell pepper,
  seeded and sliced
1 garlic clove, crushed
¼–½ teaspoon
  cayenne pepper
grated rind and juice
  of 2 limes
2 teaspoons sugar
1 teaspoon dried
  oregano
8 flour tortillas
salt and pepper,
  to taste
lime wedges,
  to garnish
salsa, to serve

1 Cut the mushrooms into slices. Heat the oil
in a large, heavy skillet. Add the mushrooms,
onion, red and green bell peppers, and
garlic and sauté for 8–10 minutes, until
the vegetables are cooked.

2 Add the cayenne pepper, grated lime rind
and juice, sugar, and oregano. Season with
salt and pepper and cook for an additional
2 minutes.

3 Meanwhile, heat the tortillas according
to the package directions. Divide the
mushroom mixture among the warmed
tortillas and roll up. Serve immediately,
garnished with lime wedges and served
with salsa.

Replace the mushrooms with strips of cooked chicken for a meaty alternative.

CHICKEN SKEWERS
(with satay sauce)

 Serves: 4

Prep: 15 mins
+ soaking

Cook: 6–8 mins

- - - - - - - - - - - - - - - - -

**4 skinless, boneless
chicken breasts,
about 5 ounces
each**
**2 tablespoons
olive oil**
**2 tablespoons
lemon juice**

Satay sauce
**½ cup smooth
peanut butter**
**1½ tablespoons
olive oil**
**2 tablespoons
hot water**
**1½ tablespoons light
soy sauce**
**2 tablespoons
apple juice**
¼ cup coconut milk

1 To make the satay sauce, mix all the ingredients together in a bowl.

2 If you are using wooden skewers, soak them in cold water for at least 30 minutes to prevent them from burning. Cut each chicken breast lengthwise into four strips and thread each strip onto a skewer.

3 Mix the oil and lemon juice together in a small bowl, then brush over the chicken.

4 Preheat the broiler to medium–high. Broil the skewers for 3 minutes on each side until golden and cooked through, making sure that there is no trace of pink inside the chicken. Serve the skewers immediately with the sauce.

Any leftover satay sauce is great for marinating chicken or turkey for a stir-fry or barbecue.

YAKISOBA

Serves: 2

Prep: 5 mins

Cook: 10 mins

1 pound ramen
   noodles
1 onion, finely sliced
2 cups bean sprouts
1 red bell pepper,
   seeded and finely
   shredded
about 1 cup sliced,
   cooked chicken
   breast
12 cooked, peeled
   shrimp
1 tablespoon oil
2 tablespoons
   Japanese soy sauce
1½ teaspoons mirin
1 teaspoon sesame oil
1 teaspoon roasted
   sesame seeds
2 scallions, finely
   sliced

1 Cook the noodles according to the package directions, drain well, and transfer to a bowl.

2 Mix together the onion, bean sprouts, red bell pepper, chicken, and shrimp in a separate bowl. Stir in the noodles.

3 Heat the oil in a wok over high heat. Add the noodle mixture and stir-fry for 4 minutes, or until golden, then add the soy sauce, mirin, and sesame oil and toss together.

4 Divide the mixture between two plates, sprinkle with the sesame seeds and scallions, and serve immediately.

If you don't have a wok, use a deep, nonstick skillet for the same stir-fried effect

SHOPPING
(ON A BUDGET)

If you want to whip up a storm in the kitchen, first you'll need to hit the stores. You may prefer to purchase a few things on a daily basis, go grocery shopping once a week, or buy in bulk during a monthly supermarket sweep. Whichever method you prefer, it is important to be careful with your budget.

Set a budget—figure out how much you can afford to spend on food and stick to that amount. Buy the essentials before splurging on treats.

Write a list—there's nothing worse than getting home and realizing that you've forgotten an important ingredient. Plus, a list should stop you from making impulse purchases that bump up your bill.

Buy loose fruit and vegetables— they are often cheaper than packaged ones. And because you're buying only as many as you need, it's less likely that you'll discover forgotten-about moldy vegetables.

Plan your meals—making a menu plan for the week ahead and buying only what you actually need (instead of what you think you need) is one of the easiest ways to cut your food bill. It doesn't have to be too restrictive; you can juggle the meals around during the week, depending on what you feel like eating—as long as you check expiration dates.

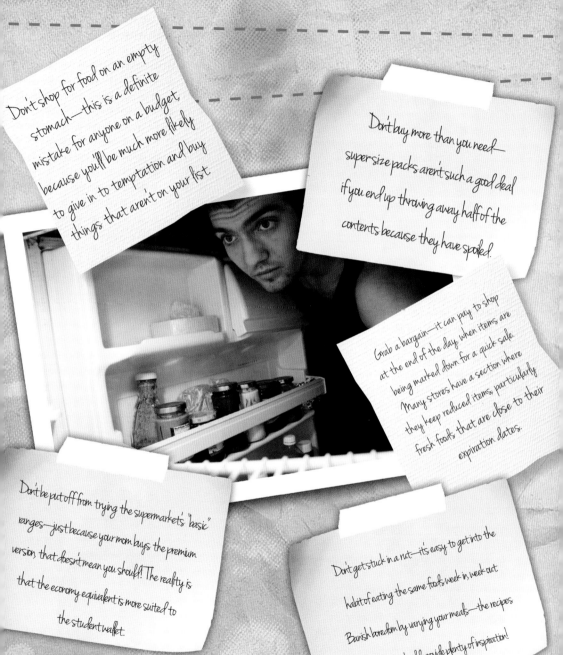

Don't shop for food on an empty stomach—this is a definite mistake for anyone on a budget, because you'll be much more likely to give in to temptation and buy things that aren't on your list.

Don't buy more than you need—super-size packs aren't such a good deal if you end up throwing away half of the contents because they have spoiled.

Grab a bargain—it can pay to shop at the end of the day, when items are being marked down for a quick sale. Many stores have a section where they keep reduced items, particularly fresh foods, that are close to their expiration dates.

Don't be put off from trying the supermarket's "basic" ranges—just because your mom buys the premium version, that doesn't mean you should! The reality is that the economy equivalent is more suited to the student wallet.

Don't get stuck in a rut—it's easy to get into the habit of eating the same foods week in, week out. Banish boredom by varying your meals—the recipes in this book should provide plenty of inspiration!

CHICKEN NUGGETS

Serves: 4

Prep: 10 mins

Cook: 10–12 mins

¼ cup dry bread crumbs
2 tablespoons finely grated Parmesan cheese
1 teaspoon dried thyme
1 teaspoon salt
pinch of pepper
2 skinless, boneless chicken breasts, cut into cubes
1 stick butter, melted
barbecue sauce or ketchup, to serve

1 Preheat the oven to 400°F.

2 Combine the bread crumbs, cheese, thyme, salt, and pepper on a large plate or in a plastic food bag.

3 Toss the chicken cubes in the melted butter, then in the bread crumb mixture. Place on a baking sheet and bake in the preheated oven for 10 minutes, until crisp and completely cooked, with no traces of pink when cut through with a sharp knife.

4 Remove the chicken nuggets from the oven and serve immediately with barbecue sauce or ketchup.

Try these chicken nuggets for a healthier, homemade alternative to a takeout favorite.

CLASSIC CHEESEBURGERS

Serves: 4

Prep: 8 mins

Cook: 12–15 mins

1¾ pounds ground
  chuck beef
1 beef bouillon cube
1 tablespoon minced
  dry onion
2 tablespoons water
4 slices Swiss,
  American, or
  cheddar cheese
lettuce leaves
hamburger buns,
  halved
tomato slices
fries, to serve

1 Place the ground beef in a large mixing bowl. Crumble the bouillon cube over the meat, add the dry onion and water, and mix well. Divide the meat into four portions, shape each into a ball, then flatten slightly to make a patty shape of your preferred thickness.

2 Preheat a ridged grill pan over high heat. Cook the patties for about 5 minutes on each side, depending on how well done you like your meat and the thickness of the patties. Press down occasionally with a spatula during cooking.

3 Put the cheese on top of the burgers after you have turned them.

4 Place the lettuce leaves on the bottom halves of the buns and top with the burgers. Place some tomato slices on top and add the bun lids. Serve immediately, with fries.

THIN CRUST PIZZA
(with veg and mozzarella)

Serves: 4

Prep: 15-20 mins + rising

Cook: 10-15 mins

Pizza crust
1¾ cups strong white bread flour, plus extra for dusting
1 teaspoon active dry yeast
1 teaspoon salt
2 tablespoons olive oil
1–1½ cups warm water

Topping
2 tablespoons olive oil
1 large onion, thinly sliced
½ small green bell pepper, seeded and thinly sliced
1 cup store-bought tomato sauce
2 tomatoes, sliced
2 ounces mozzarella cheese, sliced
2 tablespoons freshly grated Parmesan cheese
1 teaspoon chopped fresh basil
½ cup halved, pitted ripe black olives

1 Combine the flour, yeast, and salt in a mixing bowl. Drizzle with half the oil. Make a well in the center and pour in the water. Using your hands, mix to a firm dough and shape into a ball. Turn out onto a floured work surface and knead until it is smooth and elastic. Brush the bowl with the remaining oil. Put the dough back in the bowl and turn to coat with oil. Cover with a clean dish towel and let rise for 1 hour.

2 When the dough has doubled in size, punch down in it with the palm of your hand to release the excess air, then knead until smooth. Divide in half and roll into two pizza crusts. Place on a baking sheet.

3 Preheat the oven to 425°F.

4 For the topping, heat the oil in a skillet over medium–low heat, and cook the onion and bell pepper for 5 minutes, or until softened. Spread some of the tomato sauce over the pizza crusts, but do not go all the way to the edge. Top with the onion, bell pepper, sliced tomatoes, and mozzarella cheese. Spoon more tomato sauce over the pizzas, then sprinkle with the Parmesan cheese, basil, and black olives. Bake in the preheated oven for 10–15 minutes, or until the crusts are crispy and the cheese has melted. Serve immediately.

MACARONI AND CHEESE

Serves: 4

Prep: 30 mins

Cook: 10–15 mins

2½ cups milk
1 onion
8 peppercorns
1 bay leaf
4 tablespoons butter
⅓ cup all-purpose
   flour
½ teaspoon ground
   nutmeg
⅓ cup heavy cream
1¾ cups shredded
   Monterey Jack,
   American, or
   cheddar cheese
12 ounces dried
   macaroni
1 cup shredded
   Swiss, cheddar, or
   American cheese
pepper, to taste

1 Preheat the oven to 400°F. Put the milk, onion, peppercorns, and bay leaf in a saucepan and bring to a boil. Remove from the heat and let stand for 15 minutes.

2 Melt the butter in a saucepan and stir in the flour until well combined and smooth. Cook over medium heat, stirring continously, for 1 minute. Remove from the heat. Strain the milk into a bowl to remove the solids, then stir a little of the milk into the butter-and-flour mixture until well incorporated. Return the pan to the heat and gradually add the remaining milk, stirring continuously, until it has all been incorporated. Cook for an additional 3 minutes, or until the sauce is smooth and thickened, then add the nutmeg and cream and season with pepper. Add the Monterey Jack cheese and stir until melted.

3 Meanwhile, bring a large saucepan of water to a boil. Add the macaroni, return to the boil, and cook according to the package directions, or until tender but still firm to the bite. Drain well and add to the cheese sauce. Stir together well.

4 Spoon the mixture into an ovenproof dish and sprinkle with the Swiss cheese. Bake in the preheated oven for 20 minutes, until bubbling and brown. Serve immediately.

TUNA-NOODLE CASSEROLE

Serves: 4-6

Prep: 20 mins

Cook: 20-25 mins

8 ounces dried
  tagliatelle
2 tablespoons butter
1 cup fresh bread
  crumbs
1 (14-ounce) can
  condensed cream of
  mushroom soup
½ cup milk
2 celery stalks,
  chopped
1 red and 1 green bell
  pepper, seeded and
  chopped
1¼ cups shredded
  cheddar or
  American cheese
2 tablespoons
  chopped fresh
  parsley
1 (5-ounce) can chunk
  light tuna in oil,
  drained and flaked
salt and pepper,
  to taste

1 Preheat the oven to 400°F.

2 Bring a large saucepan of lightly salted water to a boil. Add the pasta and cook for 2 minutes less than the cooking time specified on the package directions. Meanwhile, melt the butter in a saucepan over medium heat. Stir in the bread crumbs, then remove from the heat and reserve.

3 Drain the pasta well and reserve. Pour the soup into the pasta pan over medium heat, then stir in the milk, celery, bell peppers, half the cheese, and all the parsley. Add the tuna and gently stir in so that the flakes don't break up. Season with salt and pepper. Heat just until small bubbles appear around the edge of the mixture.

4 Stir the pasta into the pan and use two forks to mix all the ingredients together. Spoon the mixture into an ovenproof dish and spread out. Stir the remaining cheese into the bread crumbs, then sprinkle over the top of the pasta mixture. Bake in the preheated oven for 20–25 minutes, until golden. Let stand for 5 minutes before serving straight from the dish.

This easy one-dish meal is ideal for using staples when food supplies are low, and it's cheap too!

CHILI CON CARNE

Serves: 4

Prep: 10 mins

Cook: 30–35 mins

2 tablespoons
  sunflower oil
1 pound ground
  round beef
1 large onion,
  chopped
1 garlic clove, finely
  chopped
1 green bell pepper,
  seeded and diced
1 teaspoon chili
  powder
1 (28-ounce) can
  diced tomatoes
1 (28-ounce) can
  red kidney beans,
  drained and rinsed
2 cups beef stock
handful of fresh
  cilantro sprigs,
  chopped, plus
  sprigs to garnish
salt, to taste
freshly cooked rice
  and sour cream,
  to serve

1 Heat the oil in a large, heavy saucepan or
flameproof Dutch oven or casserole dish.
Add the beef and cook over medium heat,
stirring frequently, for 5 minutes, or until
broken up and browned.

2 Reduce the heat, then add the onion,
garlic, and green bell pepper to the pan and
cook, stirring frequently, for 10 minutes.

3 Stir in the chili powder, tomatoes, and
kidney beans. Pour in the stock and season
with salt. Bring to a boil, reduce the heat,
and simmer, stirring frequently, for about
15–20 minutes, or until the meat is tender.

4 Stir the chopped cilantro into the meat.
Transfer to serving bowls and garnish
with the reserved cilantro sprigs. Serve
immediately with rice and sour cream.

SPAGHETTI WITH MEATBALLS

Serves: 4

Prep: 20 mins

Cook: 20–25 mins

1 cup fresh bread
   crumbs
1 pound ground
   round beef
4 garlic cloves,
   crushed
1 extra-large egg,
   lightly beaten
½ cup finely grated
   Parmesan cheese
flour, for coating
2 tablespoons
   olive oil
2 teaspoon dried
   oregano
1 (28-ounce) can
   diced tomatoes
1 tablespoon tomato
   paste
1 teaspoon sugar
1 pound dried
   spaghetti
salt and pepper,
   to taste

1. Place the bread crumbs in a bowl with the beef, half of the garlic, egg, and cheese and season with salt and pepper.

2. Mix the beef mixture until it comes together in a ball. Flour your hands and roll the mixture into walnut-size balls. Chill the meatballs in the refrigerator while you make the sauce.

3. Heat the oil in a saucepan and add the remaining garlic and oregano. Stir for 1 minute. Add the tomatoes, tomato paste, and sugar. Bring to a boil, then reduce the heat and simmer for 8 minutes.

4. Carefully place the meatballs in the pan and spoon the sauce over them. Cover and simmer for 20 minutes, turning the meatballs occasionally.

5. Meanwhile, bring a large saucepan of lightly salted water to a boil. Add the spaghetti, return to a boil, and cook according to the package directions, or until tender but still firm to the bite. Drain and serve immediately with the meatballs and tomato sauce.

NO-BAKE CHOCOLATE CAKE

Serves: 6-8

Prep: 10 mins
+ chilling

Cook: No cooking

8 ounces semisweet
  chocolate, broken
  into pieces
2 sticks unsalted
  butter
3 tablespoons
  black coffee
¼ cup firmly packed
  light brown sugar
few drops of vanilla
  extract
2 cups crushed
  graham crackers
½ cup raisins
¾ cup chopped
  walnuts

1 Line an 8½-inch loaf pan with parchment
paper. Melt the chocolate, butter, coffee,
sugar, and vanilla extract in a saucepan over
low heat.

2 Stir in the crushed graham crackers, raisins,
and walnuts and stir well. Spoon the batter
into the prepared loaf pan.

3 Let set for 1–2 hours in the refrigerator,
then turn out and cut into thin slices
to serve.

Chocolate cake doesn't get any easier than this—keep chilled in the refrigerator for a quick chocolate fix

PEANUT BUTTER COOKIES

Makes: 28

Prep: 12 mins

Cook: 12–15 mins

1 stick butter,
  softened, plus
  extra for greasing
½ cup chunky
  peanut butter
½ cup granulated
  sugar
½ cup firmly packed
  light brown sugar
1 egg, beaten
½ teaspoon vanilla
  extract
¾ cup all-purpose
  flour
½ teaspoon
  baking soda
½ teaspoon
  baking powder
pinch of salt
1¼ cups rolled oats

1 Preheat the oven to 350°F. Grease two large baking sheets.

2 Place the butter and peanut butter in a bowl and beat together well. Beat in the granulated sugar and brown sugar, then gradually beat in the egg and vanilla extract.

3 Sift the flour, baking soda, baking powder, and salt into the mixture, add the rolled oats, and stir until just combined.

4 Place spoonfuls of the dough onto the prepared baking sheets, spaced well apart to allow for spreading. Flatten slightly with a fork.

5 Bake in the preheated oven for 12 minutes, or until lightly browned. Let the cookies cool on the baking sheets for 2 minutes, then transfer to a wire rack to cool completely before serving.

44

Try crumbling these cookies over ice cream with some hot chocolate sauce for a super speedy dessert with a nutty kick.

BAKED BANANAS
(with chocolate sauce)

Serves: 2

Prep: 5 mins

Cook: 10–12 mins

- 2 small bananas
- 4 teaspoons light corn syrup
- 2 tablespoons unsweetened cocoa powder

1 Preheat the oven to 350°F.

2 Bake the bananas in their skins for 10 minutes, or until the skins are black.

3 Meanwhile, warm the corn syrup in a small saucepan over medium heat for 2–3 minutes. Stir in the cocoa powder until smooth and the consistency is like chocolate. Keep warm.

4 When the bananas are cooked, discard the skins and put the flesh onto plates. Pour the chocolate sauce over the bananas and serve immediately.

This dish is great for using up any leftover (and slightly squishy) bananas.

apples
  Apple pancakes 10–11
Apple pancakes 10–11
avocado 18

Baked bananas 46–47
bananas 46

beans
  bean sprouts 24
  red kidney 38
  refried 16
beef
  Chili con carne 38–39
  Classic cheeseburgers
    30–31
  Spaghetti with
    meatballs 40–41
bell peppers
  green 18, 32, 36, 38
  red 14, 20, 24, 36
  roasted 16
buns, hamburger 30
butter, maple syrup 10

carrots 14
celery 36
cheese 12, 16, 28, 30,
  32, 34, 36, 40
chicken
  Chicken nuggets 28–29
  Chicken skewers 22–23
  Yakisoba 24
Chicken nuggets 28–29
Chicken skewers 22–23
Chiles 16, 38
Chili con carne 38–39
Chive scrambled
  eggs 8–9

chocolate 42
  sauce 46
Classic cheeseburgers
  30–31
coleslaw 12
cookies 42, *see also*
  Peanut butter
    cookies

Deli-style sandwiches
  12–13

eggs 6, 8, 10, 40, 44

fries 30

hummus 14

lettuce 30

Macaroni and cheese
  34–35
mushrooms 6, 20

Nachos 16–17
No-bake chocolate cake
  42–43
noodles 24
nuts 42

olives 32
onions 20, 24, 30, 32,
  34, 38

pasta 18, 36
  Macaroni and cheese
    34–35

Pasta salad 18–19
Spaghetti with
    meatballs 40–41
Pasta salad 18–19
Peanut butter cookies
  44–45
pesto 18
pimentos 16
pita bread 14

Satay sauce 22
scallions 24
shrimp 24
Spaghetti with
    meatballs 40–41
spinach, leaf 14
Sunshine toast 6–7

Thin crust pizza 32–33
tomatoes 6, 18, 30, 32,
  38, 40
tortillas 16, 20
tuna
  Pasta salad 18
  Tuna-noodle casserole
    36–37
Tuna-noodle casserole
  36–37
turkey
  Turkey salad pita
    pockets 14
Turkey salad pita pockets
  14–15

Vegetable fajitas 20–21

Yakisoba 24–25
yogurt 18